THE ART
OF
TREMENDOUS

Ten Tips for Life

Dr. Tracey C. Jones

TREMENDOUS LEADERSHIP

Leadership with a kick!

Tremendous Leadership
PO Box 267 • Boiling Springs, PA, 17007
(717) 701 - 8159 • (800) 233 - 2665 •
www.TremendousLeadership.com

Tremendous Leadership's titles may be bulk purchased for business or promotional use or for special sales. Please contact Tremendous Leadership for more information.

Paperback ISBN: 978-1-961202-04-7
eBooks ISBN: 978-1-961202-05-4

DESIGNED & PRINTED IN THE
UNITED STATES OF AMERICA

DEDICATION

To my father, Charles, who taught me that a tremendous life is the only life worth living, and to my mother, Gloria, whose love and support enabled Tremendous to be tremendous. And to all of you who have diligently supported the work he started and enabled me to continue. Thank you for loving me as much as you loved them. This work is especially written for you.

TABLE OF CONTENTS

THANKFULNESS
READING
EXPERIENCE
MARRIAGE
ENTHUSIASM
NOTHING WORKS
DISCIPLINE
OBSTACLES
UNDERSTANDING
SAVIOR

TEN TIPS FOR LIFE

KEEPING UP WITH THE JONES

I often joke that being raised by a motivational speaker was a cross between boot camp and a sitcom. Growing up with Charlie "Tremendous" Jones as a father was a brilliant blend of focus and fun, discipline coupled with daydreaming, and laughter followed by reflection. I still receive letters, emails, texts, and calls from individuals reflecting on my father's impact on their lives.

An individual once asked me a question that had such an impact that it became the impetus for this book. The context occurred while I was an officer in the United States Air Force, and my father was speaking close to my duty station. I loved it when his meetings were scheduled near my assignments, as I had the chance to see one or both of my parents and experience the art of being tremendous.

Sitting in the audience and observing the reactions to his words was one of the activities I enjoyed most. It's like watching your favorite movie with a friend who has never seen it. You know all the funny stories that will make them double over with laughter. You also know the poignant parts that will cause them to reach for tissues to wipe away a tear. You get to sit back and watch the words wash over them, encouraging their spirits.

After those meetings, people would chat and network. A man approached me and asked a simple but compelling question, "Is he always like that?" Now, you cannot hear the tone in which this was asked, so I will tell you. It was not a tone of sarcasm or denigration; it was earnest and incredulous. And if you had the blessing of watching my father on stage, you would understand why; he had an unsurpassed star quality. It was a question a genuinely exhausted listener, whose side hurt from laughing, whose eyes were swollen from tearing up, or who got manhandled while sitting in the front row would honestly ask.

I paused, thought momentarily, and said, "Why yes, he is." It has been 15 years since Tremendous triumphantly entered the gates of heaven. And if he were still with us today, he would be overjoyed at the number of dear brothers and sisters living transformed lives because of "the people they meet and the books they read." This reality proves that although the man is gone, what made the man is as accessible, abundant, and relevant today as ever.

So I hope you enjoy this summary of all things Tremendous. And what better way to package it than in the acronym **TREMENDOUS!** I knew my father when he was on this earth, but I truly got to know him in a different, deeper, and more meaningful way after he departed. I'm excited to share what I've discovered by combing through countless writings, scribbles, recordings, Bibles, stories, and love notes—what makes someone genuinely tremendous.

When I returned to run Executive Books in 2009, I knew I could never fill his shoes, nor did I want to. He, like each of us, was one of a kind. But 15 years later, the principles he taught can be used by anyone, anywhere, at any time. These ten ingredients are a surefire recipe for an extraordinary life. May this book serve as a reminder that life is still tremendous; then and now!

TREMENDOUS
THANKFULNESS

*"Let an attitude of gratitude flavor
everything you do."* – CTJ

My father entered this world in 1927, the
first of five children. The global financial
collapse that began two years later set the
stage for the world he would grow up in.
As a young adult conscious of the impact of
economics and development, I always sensed
that my father didn't have it easy growing
up. However, he never dwelt on the negative
aspects. Instead, I heard stories about
how his father worked any job he could to
provide for them.

*"Like so many children born into
poverty, I was blissfully unaware of
our status until I was old enough to*

realize that our family differed from others. No one has the privilege to choose their country, their parents, or the circumstances they grow up in. As for our family, we lived in a back alley structure with no electricity or indoor plumbing." – Charlie "Tremendous" Jones, *It's All About Jesus*

Like his father, young Charles worked several jobs as a pre-teen to help support his family, and the long hours took a toll on his schoolwork. At the close of 8th grade, the instructor told him he would have to repeat the academic year. Charlie chose to drop out of school and work as a laborer with his father. When I share this fact, I have had numerous friends tell me the same about their tremendous fathers! In the past, dropping out of school was not the setback for young men and women as it is today. Back then times were tough; education was a luxury, and every able body had to work to put food on the table.

However, young Charlie never let that stop him from being thankful. He was aware that others had more than he did, but it never entered his mind that they were poor or lesser than the other boys. Throughout his life, Charlie was aware of the kindness of strangers, of the anonymous donors who filled their home with Christmas presents when his father was too broke and unable to secure a loan with the bank. He was grateful to his neighbors who took the time to bring him to Sunday School and model the love of God. He cherished my mother, Gloria, who said 'yes' to an unknown boy at a Franklin and Marshall prom he crashed when he asked her to dance and marry him 13 weeks later. He respected the life insurance industry, which showed him the value of preparing for your loved ones in the event you can no longer.

He was thankful for Jim Shelley, an unknown prospect who jumped in his car to whom Charles thought he could sell an insurance policy but who introduced Charles to a relationship with Christ instead. He was grateful to the Christian Business Men's Connection (CBMC), who discipled him and helped him grow in his faith and fullness in Christ. He felt blessed by a country that allowed a boy with nothing to achieve more than he ever dreamed of and to live, love, worship, and earn freely.

Tremendous shared this prayer before our meals:

Lord, we thank You for our food, but if we had no food, we would want to thank You just the same because we're not thankful just for what You give us but, most of all, for the privilege of learning to be thankful.

For many years, I had a difficult time processing what he meant. But now I am beginning to realize that we are to give thanks for everything. Yes, even in the turmoil and things I disagree with, because the only thing that matters, in the end, is a grateful heart and the privilege of learning to be thankful.

Upon coming home in 2009, I got to pour through my father's records and files. I found evidence of many things that a business owner, partner, or parent would not consider something to be thankful for. I was stunned at the amount of wrongdoing and heartache my father endured. Yet I never heard him complain about any of these, not one word. In fact, I only learned about many of them when going through his files years later. His responses were always oriented toward giving gratitude and praise regardless of the circumstances. Thankfulness is the bedrock for mastering the art of being tremendous because gratitude is the purest reflection of a humble heart.

TREMENDOUS TIP: Find something to be thankful for in everything that happens.

tREMENDOUS
READING

"The most tremendous experience of life is the learning process. The saddest time is when a person thinks he has learned enough." – CTJ

Tremendous was a book evangelist of epic proportions. He often joked that he was a "pusher" who loved to get people "hooked on books." As a young boy who flunked out of school in the 8th grade and went on to become one of the legends of personal development, he intimately knew and breathed the transformative power of books. Frequently, individuals would come to him for directional advice or crisis comfort. Instead of allowing them to engage in analysis paralysis or regurgitate self-defeating words, he would bring them into his library, tell them to select a book from his vast collection that caught their eye, open it, and read aloud for twenty minutes. No other dialogue was exchanged.

At the close of their time, the individual would look up with tears in their eyes or clarity of vision and say to my father, "How did you know that's exactly what I needed to hear?" He did the same thing with the weekly Bible studies he and my mother, Gloria, hosted in their homes. No opinions were to be shared, only answers originating in the Scriptures themselves. In the beginning, was the Word, and the Word was God (John 1:1). Tremendous understood and lived the power of words.

And he never let anyone leave his presence without books, not just one, but often a case, or two or three. He also maintained that business cards were ineffective, with most in the trash can, sometimes before you left the meeting! Instead, he urged them to include a book with their contact information. Books are a powerful calling card. A prospect may throw away or lose your business card, but they'll always remember the person who gave them a personally selected and autographed book. The expectation was that you would take these seeds and pay it forward to others who needed to have their hearts softened and tears wiped away by the pages of a book. And most of the time, he gave them away for free, maintaining that the more books he donated, the more riches he accumulated! His life revealed this truth in every area.

There's an actual name for this practice: Bibliotherapy. Bibliotherapy aims to heal by using literature to help you improve your life by providing information, support, and guidance through reading books and stories. Indeed, Tremendous would count Bibliotherapist as one of his most coveted descriptors. He constantly sent out bundles of books directed at teens, couples, business leaders, salespeople; you name it. In every interview or speech, he had stacks of books on the podium where he shared the words that changed his life so the attendees could engage in the same healing and growth. The highest compliment you could give him after his speech was to tell him how his words inspired you to begin or reengage a committed reading discipline. In short, personal development only happens when you develop the person. Books are the cornerstone, and reading is the source of all discovery and vision.

In addition to encouraging reading books, he also advocated that everyone should write one. After all, everyone has been put on this earth to go through specific circumstances. It is our duty to each other to record these as a beacon of light, a milestone marker of progress, a helping hand to others in the valleys. I've spent the last fifteen years of my professional life discovering and archiving my father's unpublished writings. I am thankful that he wrote throughout every aspect of his earthly and spiritual journey, not just to give God the glory for the ascent to the mountaintop, but to re-read for encouragement in the depths of the valley. Tremendous had volumes of notes, excerpts, scribbled thoughts, and typed vignettes, all born from something he had read. All tremendous communicators are voracious readers.

Growing up with a parent who was a bookaholic inevitably impacted me. I often joke that I read *How to Win Friends and Influence People* before *The Poky Little Puppy*. Televisions vanished from living areas and were packed away in the attic during my teen years so I could focus on school, athletics, work, or reading. Although I had jobs after school and during summer, my father encouraged me to earn extra money by writing one-page book reports. He began this trend with my brother Jere, a newly licensed teenager wanting a car. Charlie told Jere, "If you read in style, you'll drive in style; but if you read like a bum, you'll drive like a bum." My father always joked that overnight Jere developed a fantastic hunger for reading!

The pattern started between a father and his son impacted their ability to stay connected and communicate in the years to come.

When Jere departed for college, he would write my father a daily postcard with a thought and accompanying reflection he had read and seen come to fruition. I have hundreds of these "Dear Dad" postcards; my father's keepsake of them in the decades to come showed how much they meant to him.

The times in my life when I have been the most defeated, angry, and foolish have been when my reading was of poor substance, lacking, or non-existent. Everything begins with the power of thought; there is no activator or rejuvenator like reading beautiful books. The world works hard to tell you otherwise, but great books remind you that truth is eternal and immutable. We don't just read to be "in the know," but to be "in the grow." Tremendous often closed his meetings with a pile of books on the podium and in each hand with these words:

Don't read to be smart; read to be real.
Don't read to be big; read to be down

to earth. Don't read to memorize; read to realize. Don't read to learn; read sometimes to unlearn. And don't read a lot; read just enough to keep yourself hungry and curious and getting younger as you're growing older. **Read.**

TREMENDOUS TIP: For a more tremendous life, read tremendous books and meet tremendous people.

TR**E**MENDOUS
EXPERIENCE

"My best lessons in life are not those teaching me new things so much as those helping me unlearn some old things." – CTJ

One of the most accessible keys to building a tremendous life is experience. Experience is the most valuable resource a person can have; it trumps even birthright, upbringing, and talent. Every opportunity comes wrapped in the form of an experience. The trouble is experience is scary; it evokes feelings of hardship, potential failure, and work. Opportunity is sexy; it promises success and power. But the fact is, you can only have one with the other.

Many today are programmed to be resentful because they've been told that opportunities only go to the privileged. That's a lie. My father had no lineage on which to claim special status. Even if he did, he would have rejected it. He knew that a person could only be honed, broken, and raised through experiences. With so many people unwilling to step up to the plate, this is one area where we can all stand out.

When I graduated from high school, my father told me I had to go and "earn my stripes." This meant I couldn't live in his shadow or off his successes or failures. I had to go out and prove my own worth. The surest way to do this was to grow my experience bag. And so I did.

During college, my father recommended I sell books door-to-door for the Southwestern Company. He had spoken to their sales teams for years and was impressed with their product, enthusiasm, and the intense training ground they provided the college students via door-to-door selling. My father told me if I could do a cold call, knock on a door, and present my product, that would be one of the hardest things I would ever master.

Sign me up! Let's get the hard stuff out of the way early in life so I can get all the tough lessons behind me! He also told me that when they opened the door, put my head through it and not my foot, so if they tried to shut it, I could keep talking! You have no idea how many times that made me laugh instead of cry when I got the door slammed in my face.

A few years later, my father returned from giving a talk at New Mexico Military Institute in Roswell, NM. He laid a brochure on the kitchen table and told me, "Tracey, those kids are really going to do something with their lives." Next thing you know, I applied and got accepted. I knew I was open to saying 'yes' if my father said to do something. It's a lesson that served me well in life.

Tremendous never focused on the outcome, only the willingness. He knew that most of the time, things would go wrong, and we could be defeated. That didn't matter. What mattered was you tried, stood up, went into battle, and earned your stripes. And when you get back up after getting knocked down or set back, you don't start from zero; you start from experience.

Experience is the most valuable commodity on planet Earth. When you've got experience, you can do anything because you've got seasoning and skills. You've been battle-tested and are wise. So when there is an opportunity, someone asks if you will take on a role or position, or even if they don't ask... step up and just say yes.

In his best-selling book, *Life is Tremendous*, my father used a powerful metaphor that stuck with me throughout my life. He outlined it as one of the 7 Laws of Leadership: *Exposure to Experience*. God gives every person a psychological key ring at the beginning of life. And He provides a law that says, "Every time you expose yourself to another situation, I'll give you another key of experience for your key ring." In fact, the bad experience gives you double the keys! Soon the key ring begins filling with experiences, and then we begin to know how to pick the right key to unlock our situation.

And the more keys you have, the more extraordinary your life is. You have confidence, discernment, and wisdom. A wise friend once said, "You must start with the bad to get to the good." Experience is the only path that can get you there. This is an exciting law because its practice makes things get better and better with added years. As you accumulate experiences, you use those keys over and over again. The greatest motivations I've had have come from my own heart and home. Someone else's experience or story can never motivate you as deeply as yours.

Eventually, you know which keys unlock the doors, and you slip through while the inexperienced people search feverishly to see if they have a key. Those of us on the back nine of life learning the law of Exposure to Experience don't require the stamina we once needed; we know how to get to the heart of a problem and prescribe a remedy. This is why we see men and women in their 70s, 80s, and well into their 90s still making an incredible impact in the world. They have mastered this tremendous tool.

TREMENDOUS TIP: Grow your Experience keyring and watch what happens!

TRE**M**ENDOUS
MARRIAGE

"The success of a person in business or any other endeavor is never determined by aptitude, by the boss or by friends. Success is achieved through making a decision, making it yours and dying by it." – CTJ

To live a tremendous life, wholehearted commitment is essential. Whether directed towards your spouse, yourself if you're single, your work, or your belief system, unwavering dedication and commitment are fundamental. Tremendous maintained that there were only three decisions in life, and that every other decision was a by-product due to these core foundational blocks. *The Three Decisions* are who you are going to live your life with, what you are going to live your life doing, and who you are going to live your life for. In each decision, you entered into a covenantal relationship—a promise to abide by certain behaviors and loyalties. You had to go all in with your commitment, or else you were just trading time for money, waiting for a better mate, or being double-minded. You had to unconditionally stick with your decision when the going got rough. You had to stake your life partner, livelihood, and eternal security in these three choices.

Many people today walk away from a job or a relationship because they feel they are not getting what they deserve. In doing this, they're actually diluting the little bit of commitment they have left. Here's what Tremendous had to say about that:

"True love and commitment are learning to give whether you get anything or not! If you ever give something to get something, you're not giving in the true sense of the word;

you're trading! We don't know much about giving. Do you realize one of the significant problems in marriage is that we know so little about giving? We know all about trading but not giving. If a person is learning to give, whether he gets anything or not, he is really giving. And if you give—whether you get anything or not—you always get a greater capacity to give.

How's your Total Commitment? Have you checked it lately? If you have some and you've been using it, you're getting more. You're losing it if you have some and are not using it. I tell young men, 'If you're ever asked to take on a sideline— something more than what you've put your hand to—demand a fortune for it!' Because if you give up your small amount of total commitment, you're bankrupt. A sideline is a slide-line; whatever your hand finds to do, do it with all your might. If you use your total commitment, you'll get more, and more total commitment will get things you really want."

When Tremendous found the life insurance industry, he went all in. His best-selling book, *Life is Tremendous*, contains much of his early years of building his business and developing his team. My father reflected that he didn't find insurance; it found him. And when it did, he went all in. During his first five years in selling, one of his achievements was five years of consecutive weekly production. This means that he never missed one week in selling a policy. This sounds impressive, but it's only part of the truth. According to Tremendous,

"The whole truth is that I believed in goals and so I vowed to sell a policy every week or buy one. Let me tell you, after I bought 22 policies, I began to get motivated! Little did I realize that a simple vow would significantly influence my work for the rest of my life.

Because of that vow and what it cost me to keep it, I began to learn involvement and commitment. Some people get involved with their work but are not committed. Others are committed but don't get deeply involved. The two go together, and I'm convinced there is only one way to learn to be motivated by being totally involved and committed to whatever you are engaged in!"

Tremendous lamented that too many of us are taught that a successful marriage depends on compatibility. His response was, "Compatibility! If a successful marriage is based on compatibility, I must be the most miserable married man around!" But when he stood up and took that marriage vow, he swore off every other woman on the planet and dedicated himself wholly and solely to Gloria Burkhart Jones, for better or worse, for richer or poorer, in sickness and health.

That's the definition of unconditional love; it's love that does not hinge on conditions. When you engage in marriage to your spouse, your work, and your faith, you are committed. Commitment is learning to give whether you get anything or not. And if you give—whether you get anything or not—you always get a greater capacity to give. Take a vow, make a marriage, and commit your life to living it through. Sign that offer letter, make a career, and commit to furthering the organization's vision. Know what you believe and why, so you can live peacefully and purposefully.

TREMENDOUS TIP: Don't worry about being of more use where you aren't; the best job or relationship you'll ever have is the one you're in.

TREM**E**NDOUS
ENTHUSIASM

"I'm convinced that there is nothing that will brighten the atmosphere of a business, church or home like an enthusiastic person who offers a few positive words to others." – CTJ

There's a term in leadership literature called emotional contagion, which involves the spontaneous spread of emotions and behaviors. Tremendous understood this fact. The tagline for *Life is Tremendous* is *Enthusiasm Makes a Difference*. He knew enthusiasm was the secret sauce that made every interaction dreamy and every chore delectable. This is one of the most powerful tools for being tremendous and is equally available to each of us. We just have to commit to dialing in our emotions.

Tremendous maintained that life isn't fair, times are tough, and some rain must fall on each life. He lived this truth from an early age, undoubtedly influencing his sense of pragmatism and stoicism. He went on to say that everyone at some time is miserable. But the key is you can be 'happy miserable' or 'miserable miserable.' Your circumstances or outcomes do not have anything to do with your sense of enthusiasm. Your attitude and mindset are the only things entirely within your control. So regardless of the negativity around us, we get to choose to live positively. And since emotions are contagious and spread, we can bring light into our spaces and begin shining it into others.

Tremendous preached from the pulpit of intrinsic motivation, meaning that we control our reactions and destiny. All events happen for us and not to us. And it is up to each of us to maintain the thoughts we think, the words we speak, and the actions we take. We hear a great deal about culture in today's world.

My father described it using the word ATMOSPHERE. And as we know from the world's creation, atmosphere doesn't come out of nothingness or thin air; somebody has to create it. You are the thermostat that walks into any room. To warm it up, you have to generate the energy.

He also had some great tools to get the atmosphere fired up. My father had a beautiful habit of uttering a simple phrase whenever he interacted with or passed by someone. He would thank them for their smile. If I heard it once, I heard it a million times. "Thank you for your smile! Thank you for your smile! Thank you for your smile!" Now you may wonder what he did when someone wasn't smiling. He'd thank them anyway, maintaining that they would often give him a smile back because they didn't want to cheat him out of something he thanked them for!

So what does this simple interaction do? Why does it work? When you walk through a hallway, enter a room, or move from one airport terminal to another, and you take the time to consciously look directly at the people in your vicinity, smile at them, and recognize them, the results are incredible. In a world where people feel increasingly alone, unseen, and unworthy, Tremendous tapped into a brief moment of genuine love and respect for his brother or sister.

The other way Tremendous created atmosphere was with his humor. His energy and storytelling persona made him a natural, but I can attest that he was a voracious researcher and collector of jokes. He had files of them. He'd record and practice a good one when he heard it. He even published a book that had all of his jokes in it titled, *Humor is Tremendous*, to help those who didn't consider themselves funny. And he always had a point. He'd have you laughing so hard you couldn't breathe, and then he'd drive home a point.

Because just like emotions are contagious, so is laughter. Humor has a powerful way of uniting us; those released endorphins help create the atmosphere. For those of you who have been in a group where the speaker tells a phenomenal story or delivers the best punchline ever, you know there's nothing better than laughing out loud together.

TREMENDOUS TIP: Cultivate the habit of saying something positive to everybody.

TREMENDOUS
NOTHING WORKS

"My plan is that anything that can go wrong will go wrong. So when something goes wrong, I can say: That's my plan! You say, 'What if something goes right?' That's ok; I can work it in!" – CTJ

One of the most viewed clips of Tremendous' speeches contains his funniest line ever. The context goes like this: Tremendous builds up the audience as only he can do, telling them he will reveal the most potent truth he had learned in thirty-plus years of running a business. He then cups his hand around the microphone, leans back, and exclaims, "NOTHING... WORKS!!" Then he follows up with an equally resounding caveat, "UNLESS YOU WORK IT!"

"Nothing works unless you work it." This reality is a respecter of none. It's true whether you're young or old, rich or poor, black or white, religious or agnostic, liberal or conservative. There are two things we cannot do for people. We cannot want a thing more for them than they want it for themselves, and we cannot do the work they need to do to achieve it. We enable learned helplessness when we circumvent this truth and swoop in to pick up the pieces and try to put their lives together.

Persistence is born out through the reality that unless I do what I need to do and not what I like and want to do, my life will not yield the harvest I am looking for. The Bible states that faith without works is dead. So if you're giving up, it's because what you say you value is not what you really love. So it's time to get honest with ourselves. A tremendous life is an honest life.

Tremendous referenced this truth in another of his 7 Laws of Leadership, *Production to*

Perfection, which states we will never get things perfect this side of heaven. However, we are to continue forging forward, tweaking our old plan, and fusing whatever didn't work to create a new plan that does work. When things don't work, I don't get upset; I smile because I know this is all part of the plan. Life becomes infinitely more tremendous once we learn that NOTHING WORKS UNLESS YOU WORK IT. I own everything, my effort, my failures, my successes, my pivots, my destiny.

Tremendous said it best,

Now, I believe in doing things right. In fact, one of my frequent prayers, the cry of my heart, is 'Oh God, let me do one thing right before I die.' But I add, 'In the meantime, Lord, help me do something!' There's a law that says if you're not learning to make something happen today, you will know very little about perfection tomorrow. As a young salesman, I was learning this every step of the way. As a husband, father, Sunday school teacher— you name it—my heart delighted in doing something because while it might have been better had I waited a little longer, many of those somethings might not have been done at all.

The other brilliant principle about this statement is that it shuts down the "life's not fair" excuse. Of course life's not fair. Whoever told you it was? Again, this truth is universal. But you pick yourself up and get back in the game because the only alternative is lying down and dying. I remember one of my father's best lines, "Ever notice how many people walk around dead long before they're buried? But thank God He made it so we don't stink 'til we're in the ground."

Persistence reveals what you value. It shows how purposeful and committed you are to the words you proclaim. If you are committed to your marriage, you'll persist in finding a way forward versus filing for divorce. If you're learning that everything at work gives you experience, you'll continue showing up and not walking off the job. In a day and age where every TikTok video is someone announcing with pride that they quit their job, my father responded perfectly, "You can't quit; you ain't done nothing yet!" So stop grousing and recording, and dig in and keep persisting. It didn't work because you didn't work it.

So when you encounter plans that go awry or never materialize, you can pivot and redesign them with a renewed sense of purpose, getting one step closer to perfection. What a tremendous way to go through life, not getting bent out of shape when NOTHING WORKS, but getting excited because it gives you another opportunity to WORK IT!

TREMENDOUS TIP: A sure-fire growth formula: cram fifty years of failure into fifteen.

TREMEN**D**OUS
DISCIPLINE

"Life isn't mainly a matter of doing what you like to do; it's doing what you ought to do and need to do!" – CTJ

One of the key tenets of emotional intelligence (EQ) is self-discipline. Those in leadership know that the ultimate goal is to develop autonomous, self-regulating team members who share the organization's vision and values. These individuals' commitment to the cause means they will work to get the job done (See section M on Marriage). Others may leave the job or quietly quit, but they stand firm.

Tremendous contended that life has cycles. Sometimes it's your best year, and the next can be your worst. Wanting to quit is a fact of life, and he freely shared that he experienced wanting to quit often. However, he maintained, you can want to quit, just don't do it! He said that truth alone made him millions. He would tell others they can think about quitting, but then they must remove that thought and get back to work. Nothing tremendous can or will happen in your life without discipline. That's why we pivot on purpose, not on pain.

In his speech, "The Price of Leadership," Tremendous distills four items you will have to face repeatedly and master to become and remain a leader. One of the four tenets is Abandonment. He claimed we need to stop thinking about what we like and want to think about in favor of what we ought and need to think about. One of the first books I read when I returned to run Tremendous Leadership was "The New Common Denominator of Success" by Albert E.N. Gray. In this Life-Changing Classic, Gray claims, "The common denominator of success—the secret of success of every person who has ever been successful—lies in the fact that he or she formed the habit of doing things that failures don't like to do." Habits are born out of discipline; tremendous habits yield a tremendous life.

I begin my day by reading a Proverb. There are 31 of them, which means I get to read the most significant leadership book of all 12 times a year. The book of Proverbs is full of wisdom about how we interact with our neighbors, government, children, spouses, employers, and even animals! Proverbs also has a great deal to say about laziness. Sluggard is used 14 times in the Bible, all in the Old Testament and all in Proverbs; none of them are flattering. That's because a lack of conscientiousness and a sense of duty is reprehensible. Laziness is one of my triggers, and I let my teammates know that I am *Slacktose Intolerant*!

Discipline is also well-researched in leadership literature. Conscientiousness is one of the critical tenets of personality as cited by The Big Five Personality construct.

Conscientiousness is a beautiful trait. Conscientiousness is seen in people who plan, follow through, and obey the rules. It is the glue that holds any and all enterprises together. Without it, things devolve into chaos, and trust evaporates. Conscientious people are not only disciplined but duty-bound. They work because they understand how important it is to the fabric of the organization and society.

As I stated earlier, my grandfather had five children during the Great Depression from 1929 to 1939. During this time, work was scarce, and unemployment was rampant. But that was never an excuse for not working, even if you did not have a formal job. Here is what Tremendous learned about the importance of discipline as a young boy:

"I'm glad I was born in time to get in on the old thing called the Depression. There was one thing that everyone was learning in those days without taking any course in psychology: the most

exciting thing in the world was to be able to work! To have a job, any kind of a job, was a privilege!"

We must show others that work is not a four-letter word; it gives an individual a sense of purpose and fulfillment and contributes to the betterment of all. Tremendous worked hard, regardless of whether he felt like it or not. Thank God for those parents who show their children a role model who works! How proud I was of him. As a young girl growing up, I watched him work relentlessly, flying from city to city, taking trains and changing in the rest rooms, and sleeping on public transport floors. There was never any talk of if he liked what he was doing; his sense of commitment and duty spoke louder than words.

Family summer vacations were spent traveling in an RV, going from city to city, loaded with luggage and cases of books, as he'd speak across North America. We learned customer service skills as we worked the book tables and how to communicate by listening to world-renowned speakers on stage. We witnessed hundreds of thousands of people gathering to learn how to build their businesses and stay motivated to continue personal development.

Work was one of the most beautiful concepts I understood as a child, not because work defines you, but because work is a privilege and joy when done for the right reasons. I learned early that work is more fun than fun, so there was no need to be dichotomous about work/life balance. Everything was spectacularly intertwined. I don't have to "get away" from anything because everything is congruent and synergistic.

Proverbs 16:27 says, "Idle hands are the devil's workshop; idle lips are his mouthpiece." To avoid this trap, I had jobs after high school, either at the Red Barn fast-food restaurant on the Carlisle Pike or Pomeroy's, the retail store in Camp Hill. As I stated earlier, if I wanted to make extra money, I could augment my earnings by writing one-page book summaries on selections mutually agreed upon. There is a copy of the reading contract in the back of *Life is Tremendous*. College breaks were filled with more opportunities to learn discipline, whether at military schools, working at Word of Life Bible camps, or selling books door-to-door with the Southwestern Company. The summer months were not a time to sleep the day away and forget everything learned throughout the year. I knew to get up and do what was required, whether I felt like it or not, regardless of the outcome. When duty came first, results would surely follow.

TREMENDOUS TIP: When done with the right motives and reasons, work is more fun than fun!

TREMEND**O**US
OBSTACLES

"Things don't go wrong and break your heart so you can become bitter and give up. They happen to break you down and build you up so that you can be all that you were intended to be." – CTJ

Leaders must be growing, and all growth is associated with growing pains. Those growing pains are often associated with failure. A young fellow asked an old-timer how he became successful. The old-timer replied, "Good judgment." The young fellow then asked, "How did you get that?" The old-timer replied, "Experience." The young fellow asked again, "How did you get that?" And the old-timer replied, "Poor judgment!"

Do you know one of the main ways a person really grows? It is by failure. It's a sure thing that's the way you grow. This is why there is wisdom with being any kind of a leader. If you're going to lead, you'll know what it is to fail. Whenever someone would alert Tremendous that they had a problem, he'd exclaim, "Of course, you've got a problem; you're not dead!"

Tremendous liked to shock people who asked him to pray for their problems. He would bow his head with them and pray their problems worsened! His reasoning was, why should he pray someone out of something God put them in to break them down and ultimately make them a better person? He joked that he was the only man in America who got cards and letters from people across the country writing and saying, "Dear Mr. Jones, please quit praying for me; I've had all I can take!"

Many consider me a happy and successful person. Yet you won't know the challenges and struggles that made me that way. You only see how I have chosen to deal with these situations. If challenges are opportunities and the path to success is through failure, why do we wallow in self-pity or run away?

The state of being 'happy miserable' takes maturity and accountability. There were times when I recounted my "poor me" situations for years to anyone who would listen. What a terrible waste of time and energy! At least half of the failures and heartaches I went through were due to my lack of strength, discipline, or willingness to follow my conscience. The other half were situations meant to teach me vital life lessons here on earth. And yes, even things that go wrong due to my shortcomings can teach tremendous life lessons. Tremendous taught us that while we can't determine when we will get kicked, we can determine which way we will go when we get kicked. There's no way to grow up without some going down. No humility without humiliation.

Weariness is another of the four tenets of leadership in "The Price of Leadership." You see, being a leader entails weariness. Anyone reading this book knows that working with people is wearisome because there will always be some who will do more, but most will do less. Why is this? It's just part of our human condition. By accepting this truth, we can keep ourselves in top form rather than wallow in self-pity, frustration, or fear.

We must embrace problems because sometime in the future, we will cross paths with someone going through the same thing, and we can impart some compassion or insights to them. Obstacles are less about you and more about using what you've been through to help others and grow as an individual. When you think of them in this light, you almost look forward to them! And while there will always be times when we want to give up and quit (that's natural), remembering this truth will ensure you never go through with it. As Tremendous always said, "You can want to quit, just don't do it."

The beauty of obstacles is that they take thumb-suckers like us with thin skins and hard hearts and turn us into sweet spirits with thick skins and soft hearts. When you're fired in the crucible of trials, all the dregs and impurities are burnt away. You come out stronger and more brilliant. Every tribulation we encounter has the seed of something great embedded. It's our job to find out what it is.

We know that when a person begins to grow, the obstacles get bigger and better. But there's excitement and progress in the struggle—and life gets easier only when you're coasting downhill. Obstacles keep you focused on your "why." The great organizations of the country and the extraordinary lives in history have been built on the answers to "Why?" You can teach someone how to do a task, but that doesn't ensure their doing it. But let them discover why, and they'll learn how despite all obstacles. The key is not how to live but why you are living. This stimulus will keep you growing. As Tremendous said, "Know-how is tremendous when you know why; know-how lets you drive it, knowing-why drives you."

No one is ever successful in being a victim. But if you look at your obstacles as a Godsend, I guarantee you that sometime in the future, you'll be a positive impact on someone who desperately needs it...including yourself.

TREMENDOUS TIP: Ask yourself, what good will come from this bad?

TREMENDOUS
UNDERSTANDING

"The horrible thing about life is hearing how wrong you are; the wonderful thing about life is seeing how wrong you are." – CTJ

Tremendous was one of the toughest men on this planet, yet he had this tender side. Many men would say he reduced them to tears with his rebuke, only to pull them in to build them up. My father knew how harsh the world was. He also loved people enough to know that not being honest with them was unconscionable. He knew what it was like to be poor, uneducated, abused, stolen from, lied to, and brokenhearted.

Tremendous understood the burdens and pain people walked around with. He was also profoundly acquainted with Christ's treatment at the hands of those he came to save. Before Christ came to earth, the prophet Isaiah said this: Jesus was "a man of sorrows, and acquainted with grief." When I would complain about something or someone being unfair or hurtful, my father would ask the same question every time, "Is what you're going through anything worse than what Jesus endured?"

There's a familiar saying: before you judge a man, walk a mile in his shoes. Tremendous translated this to mean "there can be no communication without identification." Being tremendous means you can relate to people as they are, right where they are. In 1 Corinthians 9, the Apostle Paul says, "I have become all things to all people." What an incredible definition of understanding. When people know you get them, they get you. And tough times yield tremendous fruits of the spirit: patience, persistence, and perspective. The most understanding souls always have the deepest scars.

This does not mean my father empathized with, tolerated, or enabled everyone. That's not understanding; that's condescension. He, like Paul, became a type of Christlike chameleon in that whoever he was sharing with felt a kinship, an intimate inclusivity, not a standoffish judgment or cold stare. By believing Christ was the only solution to their pain, he allowed the other divisive externals, traditions, or optics not to enter the arena. He embraced others with his heart before a word was even said. It was powerful to watch.

A classic example of how this truth was lived out happened when he traveled to speak. He would always ensure that in addition to his scheduled event, he made time to search out and speak at a church, prison, or shelter. When someone asked him how he could change settings so quickly, from a corporate boardroom to a sales meeting to a prison, he'd reply, "That's easy. We're all doing time, just in different places." As someone who engages in prison ministry, I can attest to this truth as well.

Tremendous deeply understood the bond of humanity found in all of us and threaded it through every interaction.

My father also maintained that tremendous outer dialogue is contingent on excellent inner dialogue. Your words will be sweet and nourishing when your heart and head are in the right place. Your words will poison, frustrate, and tear down if they are not. He grew a successful insurance agency and became one of the top legends of personal development not because of his slick stage persona or schtick but because he was squared away internally. He understood himself first, then he could relate to others second.

Tremendous was world-renowned for his hugs. He had free hug coupons he'd give out, and people still share them today! This interaction began as a young life insurance salesman building a business. Some leaders take building up others to a whole new level, including hugs! Tremendous knew he'd take flack for this activity, and he did, claiming whatever can be misunderstood will be misunderstood. The call came down from corporate, "What's this about Jones hugging his men?" When he tried to stop, however, it was too late. The men wouldn't let him because they were getting more love from the boss at work than their wives at home!

Many claim we live in an era where this would never be acceptable in the workplace. And in some workplace cultures, this is definitely true. However, let's continue exchanging one of the most powerful things we can share with another human being in the proper context.

TREMENDOUS TIP: The hug you give may be their hope to carry on.

TREMENDOUS
SAVIOR

*"Nothing in life can compare with
the thrill of knowing God and
knowing He knows you."* – CTJ

I remember the day I got the call from my father telling me about his cancer diagnosis. I was living in Austin, TX at the time, and I still recall the red light I was at as I tried to process the news; certain events in life you just never forget. How could this be? My father was not only a spiritual and professional giant but also a physical one. At a mere 70 years young, I could not understand how this was happening. Outside of throat surgery for his vocal cord nodules, I had never even known him to be hospitalized.

Like everything else in his life, Tremendous took the news as a blessing and continued living even more purposefully. He was already driven by an intense sense of urgency and knew that he would finish this earthly part of his journey strong; this just gave him a more definitive timeline. In fact, he looked at the diagnosis with hopeful expectation, knowing that his time on earth was ending. Paul states, "For to me to live is Christ, and to die is gain." All true Christians earnestly await the homecoming when we can leave our temporal and tarnished lives and bodies and be restored to our full glory for eternity.

Many have likened my father's worldview to that of a Stoic. Stoics adapt themselves to all situations. They are inwardly grounded despite external circumstances. That my father most certainly was. But he was so much more than being grounded. He had a personal relationship with a loving and involved God who knew, cared for, and supplied his needs. There was no toughing it out or manning up, but rather a profoundly intimate and vital walk with the Holy Spirit.

Earlier, I mentioned my father's speech, "The Three Decisions." The final decision is, who will you live your life for? Tremendous answered that question unequivocally when Jim Shelley jumped into his car in Lancaster, PA back in March of 1950. After Jim opened a Bible and had my father read several verses, he left my father alone to make the most crucial decision of his life. Tremendous recounts this entire dialogue in *Life is Tremendous*, but here is where he went all in:

I made up my mind right then I'd not eat another meal, I'd not sell another policy, I'd not talk to another person until I determined if this were true. If the Bible were not true, then I would throw it in the trash can, sleep in on Sunday mornings and save my dollar a week. But if I decided that the Bible is true, I would ask God to make me a Christian no matter what it takes or whatever a Christian is. I knew I didn't need God to be successful. I didn't need God to be an American. I didn't need God to get a wife. I didn't need God to have children. But I did need something.

Tremendous would never tell anyone what they should believe or where to go to worship. He would, however, openly impart the foundation of his worldview with unwavering conviction and inspire others to be able to do the same.

When people would call and say they were praying for his healing, he'd tell them to stop delaying his homegoing. He lived vibrantly with cancer for another 10 years until the physical toll was evident in 2008. He lost his voice and wore a patch over his eye. He continued to speak and even went overseas to continue sharing. These final times were captured in a documentary of his life titled, *A Tremendous Life: The Story of Charlie*

"Tremendous" Jones. He was as influential in his whispers as he was in his words.

I stayed by his hospice bed in our home as Gloria tended to his care, and he became a mere skeleton of the man he was. He never once complained or said a word in frustration for a life about to be cut short one week shy of 81. Tremendous knew he had run the race hard, kept the faith, and was ready to go home. He spoke of complete and blessed assurance over what would transpire as his spirit departed his body to everyone who visited him or called him on the phone.

Two days before he died, he dictated a personal section of his final book to me. The book is titled, *It's All About Jesus*, and features three authors—my father, Dr. Ken Blanchard, and Bob Phillips—sharing their conversion and love of Christ. As he spoke and I transcribed, he shared his upbringing, which I knew little about. I only knew not to ask about it since it was not pleasant. Tremendous purposely did not remain at this stage of his life once he became a new creature in Christ. He refused to dwell in his past because that wasn't his new identity.

His generation had to take abuse and hardship and turn it into victory, as the laws weren't there to advocate for children or protect them. After I captured his final words, he wept and told me he no longer had to be ashamed. I was so moved. Even though Christ had healed him from the pain of his youth, he still remembered it; he just didn't let it control him. He carried this deep wound his whole life but never gave it power by repeating it. May we all learn that when we revisit our past traumas, we provide them with space to exist in the present. Anyone who wants you to keep talking about your past, including ourselves, intends to keep you there.

The following day he squeezed my hand when I told him I was returning to run the business and told me I'd take it places he never could. That was the extent of our simple and purposeful succession planning and execution. We both knew that God would work out all the necessary details. Many people tell me how much they miss my father and realize I do too. But I know with divine certainty that his departure is temporary and live with the hope of a pledge of glorious return for all eternity. If I did not have this hope, I could never do what I do. It would be too tragic and heartbreaking.

On October 16, 2008, Charlie "Tremendous" Jones triumphantly immigrated to his eternal mansion. At his homegoing celebration, the focus was not on the remembrance of him, although all those who spoke did share their favorite memory of him. Instead, each speaker included one of my father's favorite daily devotionals from Oswald Chambers' classic, *My Utmost for His Highest.* The celebration was titled "It's All About Jesus."

A tremendous life is spent living in wonderful fellowship with our Savior, Jesus Christ. There is no doubt the first words my father heard upon entering heaven were, "Well done, my good and faithful servant; enter into the joy of our Lord," and there is no doubt that I'm one step closer to seeing him again with each passing day.

TREMENDOUS TIP: You need to know *who* you are living for before you're really living.

CONCLUSION

Now that we've covered the ten tools you can use to live triumphantly, I hope you now see that you can be as tremendous as Tremendous! Commit to living out these powerful principles and watch how your life, and those around you, transforms. The ability to be tremendous is not an option but a necessity! We need to be the salt and light in a dark and dying world and give hope to future generations. For those of us who long to be tremendous, there is a way rooted in humility, endurance, and abandonment.

I am so blessed to continue living out these truths. Had my father just left a record of accomplishments or a bank account with money, I would not have been able to come back to run the company. It would have been all about him, and it would have been over when he departed. But he left me, and each of you, a way to live out these ten truths daily and victoriously. Thank you to everyone whose support enables me to continue this work! Our tremendous tribe continues to show others the way and share the eternal message of genuine hope. The art of tremendous is alive and well, and you are a part of it!

ABOUT TREMENDOUS

Recently named one of the top 25 Legends of Personal Development, Charlie "Tremendous" Jones' legacy spanned more than half a century, and his book, 'Life is Tremendous,' has sold millions of copies. Over 6,000 audiences throughout the world have laughed while listening to Charlie Jones share his ideas about life's most challenging situations in business and at home.

Known by his "Tremendous" nickname and humor, he is a recipient of the CPAE designation and the prestigious Cavett Award from the National Speakers Association. Charlie Jones entered the insurance business at the age of 22 with one of America's top ten companies. At age 23, he was awarded Mutual of New York's (MONY) most valuable associate award. Ten years later, he received his company's management award for recruiting and business management.

At age 37, his organization exceeded $100 million in sales, at which time he founded Life Management Services, Inc. to share his experience through seminars and consulting services. After his passing in October 2008, his daughter Tracey took up the mantle of leadership and continued the "Tremendous" legacy. Charlie is best remembered for his mantra, "You'll be the same person five years from now that you are today, except for two things: the people you meet and the books you read." His legacy continues to be shared around the world and is impacting the next generation of leaders.

BOOKS BY CHARLIE "TREMENDOUS" JONES

Being Tremendous: The Life, Lessons, and Legacy of Charlie "Tremendous" Jones

Books are Tremendous

Forgiveness is Tremendous

Humor is Tremendous

Kids are Tremendous

Life is Tremendous: Enthusiasm Makes the Difference

The Key to Excellence

The Love of God

El Amor de Dios

The Mystery of Self-Motivation

The Price of Leadership

The Three Decisions

The Three Therapies

It's All About Jesus: Three Bestselling Authors, One Dynamic Savior

The Tremendous Power of Prayer: A Collection of Quotes and Inspirational Thoughts to Inspire Your Prayer Life

The Eternal Life Insurance Company

La Vida Eterna SEGUROS Cía.

Check out all of Charlie's videos at www.youtube.com/@Tremendouslifebooks

Contact us at www.tremendousleadership.com

ABOUT THE AUTHOR

Author, publisher, speaker, veteran, podcaster, and international leadership expert, Dr. Tracey C. Jones is the President of Tremendous Leadership and T3 Solutions, Inc. She picked up the reins from her father, Charlie "Tremendous" Jones, in 2008. Tracey is a passionate lifelong learner, and her career spans top positions in four major industries: from the military to high tech to defense contracting and publishing.

She is a graduate of the United States Air Force Academy, a decorated veteran who served in the First Gulf War and Bosnian War, earned an MBA in Global Management, and a Ph.D. in Leadership Studies through Lancaster Bible College. Tracey is also an adjunct professor at The American College of Financial Services and was awarded a Doctor of Humane Letters (honorary Ph.D.) from Central Penn College in 2017.

Tracey is the author of twelve titles, five of which are children's books that use her rescue pets to teach character development to our next generation of emerging leaders. Tremendous Leadership funds a trust that has donated over $3.8M to local homeless shelters, recovery outreach and mission groups, disaster recovery organizations, and scholarships to local colleges in the past 15 years.

She has served on numerous non-profit boards where she uses her resources to spark greatness in others. You can find her traveling the world, speaking to groups ranging from women's ministries in Africa to teaching middle schoolers in Europe, and conducting book clubs at local State Correctional Institutions (SCI). Tracey is married to a tremendous man, Mike, and enjoys the outdoors, biking, traveling, spending time with her pack of rescue pets, and giving others the tools to live a tremendous life.

BOOKS BY
DR. TRACEY C. JONES

SPARK: 5 Essentials to Ignite the Greatness Within

A Message to Millennials: What Your Parents Didn't Tell You and Your Employer Need You to Know

Beyond Tremendous: Raising the Bar on Life

Burnett or Bridgett: A Tale of Two Employees

True Blue Leadership: Top 10 Tricks from the Chief Motivational Hound

Saucy Aussie Living: Top 10 Ways to Get a Second Leash on Life

Children's Books

From Underdog to Wonderdog: Top 10 Ways to Lead Your Pack

Boxcar Indy: A Square Dog in a Round World

Boxcar Indy Goes to Doggy World

No, No, Roscoe!

Pawsitive Purrsonality Plus

Check out more at
www.youtube.com/@Tremendousleadership

Check out the Leaders on Leadership Podcast at
www.youtube.com/@Tremendousleadership/
podcasts

Contact us: www.traceycjones.com